P9-CEP-605

Helen Baker
Endowment
Presented to
Juniata College Library
by Her Family

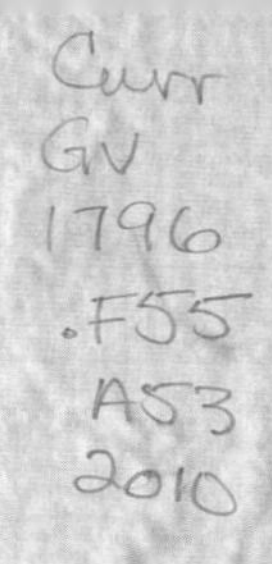

George Ancona

Lee & Low Books Inc. *New York*

¡olé! is a shout of approval and encouragement.

Many years ago I visited a small village in the south of France. I went there to see the annual gathering of the people called Gypsies. They had come from Spain and other countries in Europe to honor their patron saint, Sara-la-Kali, Sara the Black.

¡olé!

To all the *flamencos* who graciously helped make this book possible

ACKNOWLEDGMENTS
Jacket, case cover, and title page: Artwork copyright © 2010 by Pablo Ancona.
Pages 10–11: Artwork copyright © 2010 by George Ancona.
Page 12: Wood engraving "Dance of the Little Gypsies in Sacromonte" by Gustave Doré. Courtesy of The Hispanic Society of America, New York.
Page 13 top: Photograph of Gypsies dancing by Garzón. Courtesy of The Hispanic Society of America, New York.
Page 14 left: Photograph copyright © 2010 by Pablo Ancona. Used with permission.

LEE & LOW BOOKS Inc., 95 Madison Avenue, New York, NY 10016
leeandlow.com

Manufactured in China by Jade Productions, September 2010

Book design by David and Susan Neuhaus/NeuStudio
Book production by The Kids at Our House

The text is set in 12-point Shannon
10 9 8 7 6 5 4 3 2 1
First Edition

Library of Congress Cataloging-in-Publication Data
Ancona, George.
¡Olé! flamenco / George Ancona. — 1st ed.
p. cm.
Summary: "Photo-essay about Flamenco, a southern Spanish art form that incorporates song, dance, and music, tracing its cultural history and focusing on a contemporary young girl and her brother as they learn the traditional style of movement and instrument playing. Includes a glossary/pronunciation guide and author's sources"—Provided by publisher.
ISBN 978-1-60060-361-7 (hardcover : alk. paper)
1. Flamenco—History—Juvenile literature—Pictorial works. 2. Flamenco dancers—Juvenile literature—Pictorial works. 3. Flamenco music—Juvenile literature—Pictiorial works. I. Title.
GV1796.F55A53 2010
793.3'19468—dc22 2010022272

Caravans, buses, and old cars with trailers filled the streets. In between two trailers, a crowd surrounded a guitar player and a singer. Children and adults took turns dancing within the tight circle. Sometimes the spectators laughed, and at other times they were quiet. But mostly they clapped and shouted "*¡Olé!*"

I was watching flamenco, the dramatic Spanish art of song, dance, and music. When I was younger, I had studied flamenco guitar, but at this gathering I discovered the roots of flamenco—and the roots of this book.

George Ancona

Janira Cordova puts on a skirt over her pants to get ready for her flamenco class. She is the youngest in a group of dancers who study and perform Spanish dances. The dance company, in Santa Fe, New Mexico, is called Flamenco's Next Generation.

Under the guidance of their teacher, the students rehearse one of the many flamenco dances they are learning. A singer and a guitar player accompany them.

At some point during the rehearsal each dancer steps forward to do a solo. A solo is the dancer's chance to dance alone in her or his own way. While a dancer performs, the others clap to the rhythm of the music and cheer on the dancer by shouting "¡Olé!"

Children may begin taking flamenco classes when they are very young. In the studio, a guitar player provides the music while the teacher claps the rhythm and calls out the movements. By following their teacher's instructions, the students learn how to move their arms and bodies and stamp their feet. The students are working toward the day when they will dance well enough to perform before an audience on a stage with colored lights and live music.

These young dancers are learning an art that goes back a long, long time.

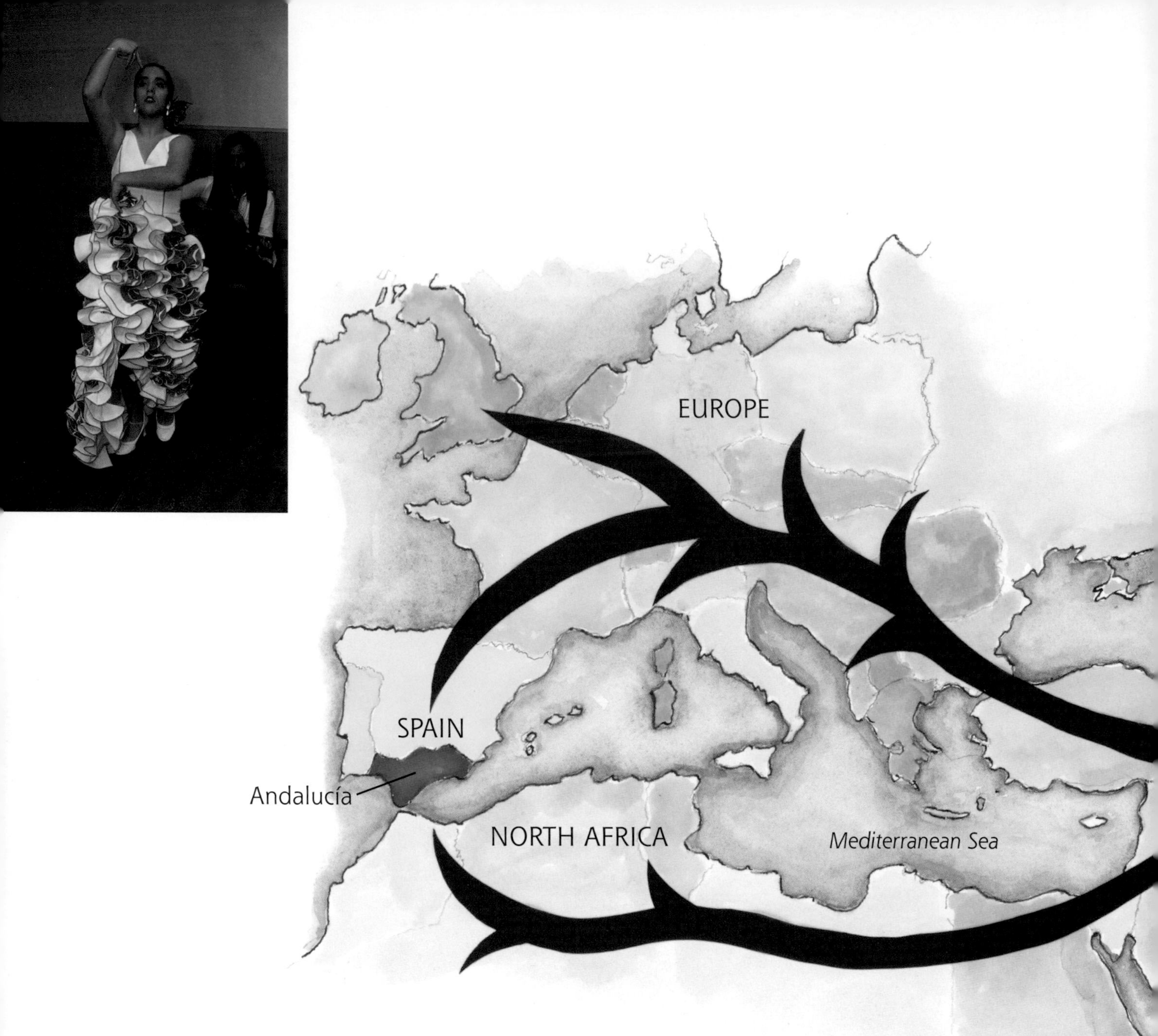

Flamenco grew out of the music and dance of the Roma, the people who came to be called Gypsies. Some legends say the Roma were from Egypt. The name Gypsy comes from *Egipto*, the Spanish word for "Egypt."

Gypsies have no written history, but historians believe that around 1000 CE the ancestors of the Gypsies fled from invasions of their homeland in northern India. They traveled with their camels and horse-drawn caravans through the Middle East, North Africa, and Europe. The people would settle in one place for a while, work, and then move on. They were animal trainers, blacksmiths, potters, fortune-tellers, and basket weavers. The Gypsies also brought with them their sense of independence, and their songs and dances.

Gypsies were outsiders wherever they went, and they were often persecuted. By the early 1400s they finally found safety in Andalucía, the southern region of Spain. The area was ruled by the Moors, who had come from North Africa hundreds of years earlier. Gypsies, Moors, Arabs, Jews, and Christians lived in Andalucía freely. The music and dances of all these peoples blended with those of the Gypsies.

In 1492 the Spanish Catholic rulers King Ferdinand and Queen Isabella reclaimed Andalucía from the Moors. People who did not convert to the Catholic religion were forced to leave. Many of the Gypsies, Moors, and Jews went into hiding in remote areas and in caves.

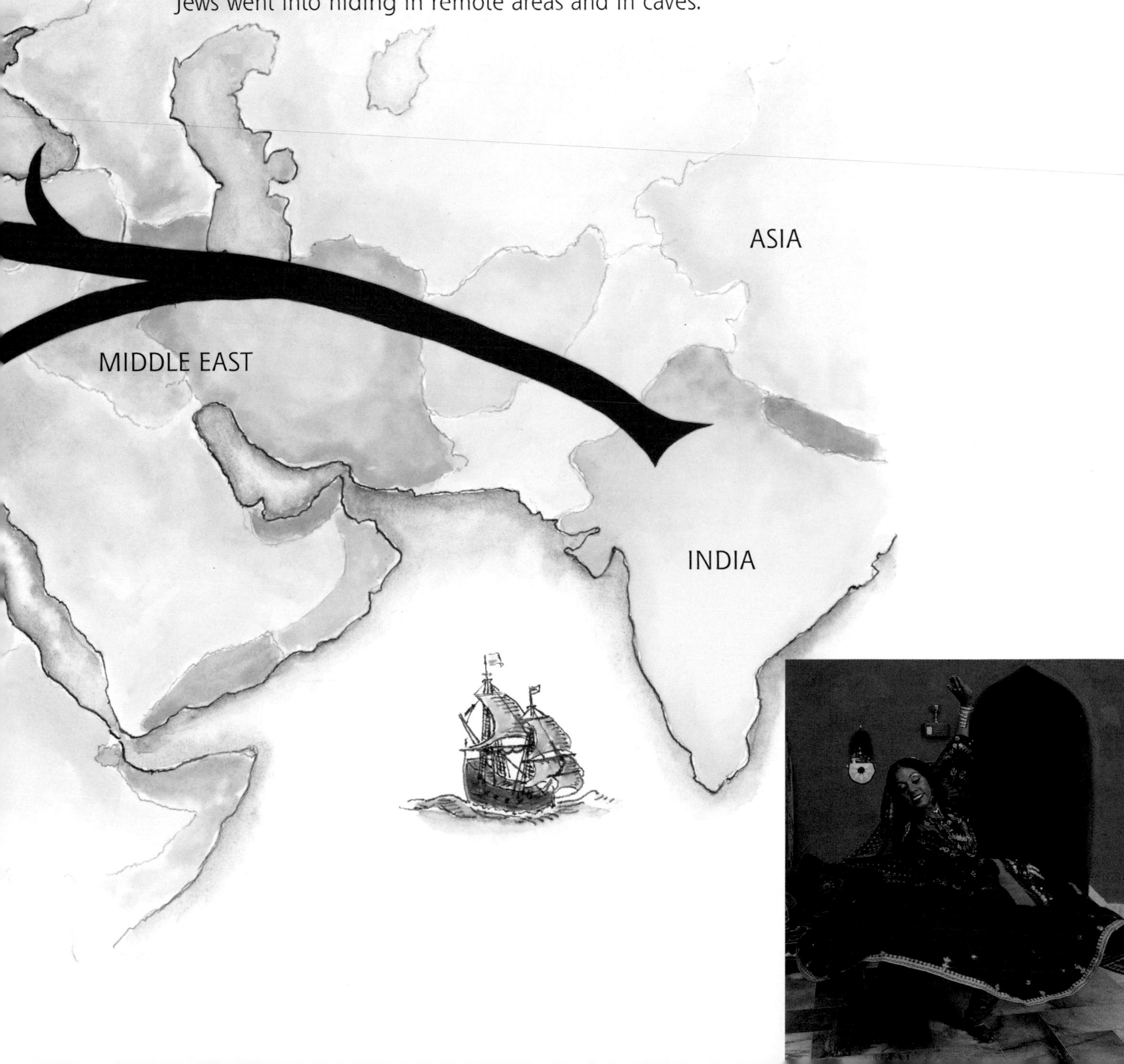

For the next three hundred years the Gypsies were continually oppressed. During this time they composed songs that told about their lives. These songs were often sung around a campfire. Eventually dancing, and then guitar playing, were added. This was the beginning of flamenco.

In the mid-1800s the French artist Gustave Doré visited southern Spain. While there he sketched Gypsies who lived in the caves of Sacromonte, a neighborhood in the city of Granada. From his sketches Doré later made engravings like this one of elders teaching children to dance.

Flamenco was originally practiced only among the Gypsies themselves. But by the beginning of the 1900s the Gypsies were performing flamenco in cave taverns and restaurants in Sacromonte. These places still exist, and visitors can see wonderful performances of flamenco there.

In Spain, flamenco is still passed down from grandparents and parents to children. In this family, Grandma, a dancer, practices flamenco steps with one of her grandsons. Grandpa, a singer, claps to teach another grandson the rhythms of the music. Papa then shows his son how to play the guitar.

And they all shout "¡Olé!" when the boy gets up to dance.

Today there are Gypsy communities in many countries, and flamenco has circled the globe. Because flamenco is a living art, it is always changing. The earliest songs were a blend of Spanish, Moorish, Arabic, Jewish, and Roma styles. Over the years musical styles and rhythms from other cultures and countries have mixed with the traditional flamenco songs and music.

People of all ages and backgrounds now study flamenco. Schools can be found across the United States and around the world. But for this family back in Santa Fe, flamenco still begins at home.

Many elements make up flamenco, but the three main parts are song, dance, and music.

When flamenco began, there was only *cante*, or song. The songs told of the joys, loves, pain, sorrow, and in some cases misery of the Gypsies' lives.

A male singer is a *cantaor*, and a female singer is a *cantaora*. The sounds that come from a singer's throat can be rough and wailing. The singers share with listeners the powerful feelings that come from deep inside them. These strong feelings that inspire a singer are called *duende*.

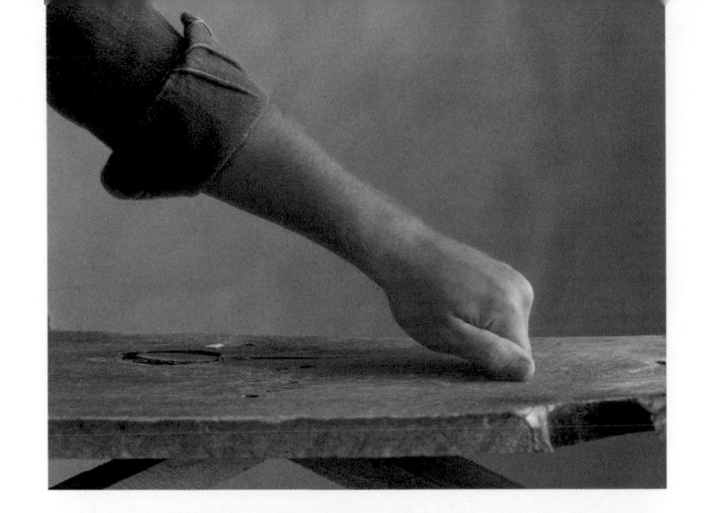

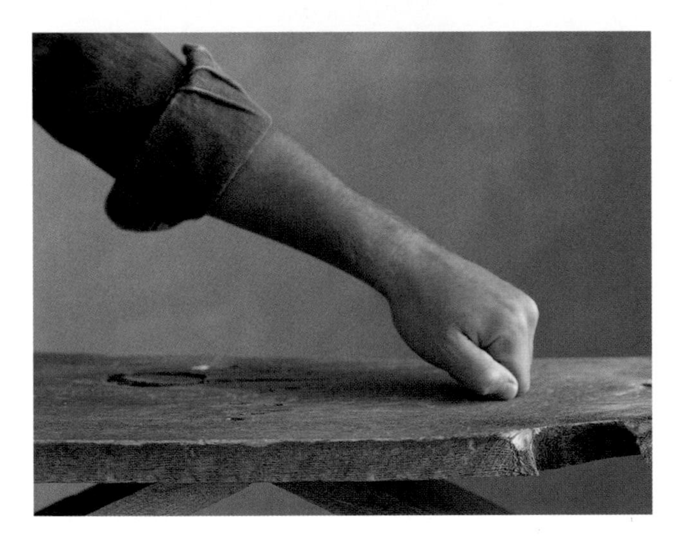

Originally a singer sang alone or was joined by someone who helped emphasize the *compás*, the beat and rhythm, of the song. This was done by hitting a stick on the floor or knocking the knuckles of a hand on a table.

A blacksmith might accompany his singing by banging a hammer on his anvil to accent the rhythm of his song.

In time people began to perform solo dances to the singing. A *bailaora*, female dancer, or *bailaor*, male dancer, needed strong, loud beats to stress the rhythm of a song. These beats were made by *palmas*, rhythmic hand clapping. Each dance has its own pattern of palmas.

The sounds of the palmas vary. When two palms are clapped together, they make a muffled sound. When four fingers of one hand strike the palm of the other hand, the sound is loud and sharp. The people who perform palmas are called *palmeros*.

Next, guitar music was added to accompany the singing and dancing. A *tocaor*, guitar player, responds to the mood created by a singer and a dancer. The singer and dancer may suddenly change the mood, so the guitarist must be able to change the way he plays quickly.

The strings of a flamenco guitar are lower and closer to the neck of the instrument than they are on other guitars. This creates a sharp sound when the guitar is played. The guitarist rapidly extends the fingers one by one across the strings. This kind of strumming is called *rasgueado*.

Nicholas, Janira's brother, is studying flamenco guitar. He learns by listening to and following the way his teacher plays. Once he learns to do what his teacher has shown him, Nicholas can begin to make changes and play the music his own way.

Another instrument used to play flamenco music today is the *cajón*, which comes from Peru. It is a wooden box with a hole cut in the back. It may also have strings inside. The musician sits on the box and slaps the front like a drum.

Adding to the sounds of the singing and the music is a dancer's *zapateado*, or footwork. The rapid stamping of the heels and thumping of the soles of the dancer's shoes on the floor become another musical instrument.

A dancer's arms create lines as they flow through space. One arm goes up as the other moves down. The arms twirl around the body and over the head.

The dancer's hands and fingers are extended and turned out like flower petals moving in the wind.

Dancers often accompany their movements by quickly snapping two fingers of each hand.

Sometimes castanets are used. The two small, shallow, wood cups are clicked together rapidly with the fingers.

A male dancer usually wears a shirt, vest, tight trousers or a suit, and boots. His movements are sharp and strong. His hands are held flat as they slice through the air and slap his feet, thighs, and chest. When he grabs the air, his hands become fists. His boots pound the floor. He may be aggressive or proud. Many of his moves look like those of a bullfighter.

A female dancer usually wears a colorful dress with a wide, ruffled skirt. The movement of a dancer's skirt is an important part of the dance. Some skirts have a long train that the dancer flicks as she moves. Or she may pick up her train to show her feet stamping the floor. The dancer's spirited dancing may express many different emotions.

A dancer's face is never still. Along with the arm, hand, and foot movements of flamenco, the face shows what the dancer feels through expressions such as a frown, a glare, or a smile.

The dancer's whole body moves to the specific rhythm of each dance. The back is arched as arms and hands reach out, up, and around the body. Skirts whirl. Feet stamp loudly on the floor. The dancer may convey the softness of a gentle breeze or the frenzy of a tornado.

After months of rehearsing, Janira and the other dancers from Flamenco's Next Generation are finally ready to perform before an audience. The girls put on makeup and their ruffled dresses. Each girl's hair is combed back into a tight bun, and a flower is tucked into the side.

Excitement is in the air as the dancers move onto the stage. The singing, music, palmas, and applause of the crowd inspire them to dance their best.

When they are not performing, the *flamencos*—singers, dancers, and musicians—and their friends sometimes gather informally. They sing, dance, and play music together. This kind of gathering is known as a *juerga flamenca*. Everyone is free to join in, share feelings, and take part in his or her own way.

Calls of "¡Olé!" ring out, and compliments fill the air.

"*¡Así se canta!*" That's singing!

"*¡Así se baila!*" That's dancing!

"*¡Así se toca!*" That's playing!

On a holiday or a weekend, Janira's family and friends like to get together to visit, eat, relax, and have fun. When the guitars appear, it is the signal for the family juerga flamenca to begin. Children, parents, uncles, aunts, grandpas, and grandmas take turns so everyone has a chance to dance in the company of loved ones.

To celebrate their heritage, the Hispanic people of Santa Fe hold a two-day Spanish Market each July. Hundreds of artists bring their carvings, paintings, tinwork, and weaving to the Santa Fe Plaza to sell. On the stage in the plaza, music and dancing entertain the visitors.

Janira and Nicholas have learned the traditional art of making *retablos*, religious paintings on wood. Their grandfather, father, and an uncle create retablos too. The men also carve and paint wooden sculptures.

The children usually sell all their retablos on the first day of the market.

Spanish Market also provides another opportunity for Janira to perform flamenco with her dance company. She changes into a long dress and her dancing shoes. Janira's mother combs back her daughter's hair and twists it into a tight bun.

Janira is ready to dance.

The plaza is filled with a crowd of shoppers, tourists, and families. The singers and guitar players sit in a semicircle onstage. Applause and welcoming voices greet the dancers as they file onto the stage.

The singers begin to sing, and the palmeros join in. The guitarists start to play. And then the dancers burst into dance. Flowing arms are held high. Fingers snap. Skirts spin. Feet stamp rapidly. One by one, each dancer moves to the front of the stage to dance a solo. As Janira looks out at the cheering crowd, she seems to say, "This is me. My dance is a gift to you."

¡olé! flamenco!

Glossary and Pronunciation Guide

Andalucía (ahn-dah-loo-SEE-ah; *in Spain*: ahn-dah-loo-THEE-ah): region in southern Spain

¡Así se baila! (ah-SEE seh BYE-lah): That's dancing!

¡Así se canta! (ah-SEE seh CAHN-tah): That's singing!

¡Así se toca! (ah-SEE seh TOH-cah): That's playing!

bailaor (bye-lah-OHR): male flamenco dancer

bailaora (bye-lah-OHR-ah): female flamenco dancer

bailaores (bye-lah-OHR-ehs): flamenco dancers, all males or males and females

cajón (kah-HOHN): wooden box drum with a hole cut in the back; may also have strings inside

cantaor (kahn-tah-OHR): male flamenco singer

cantaora (kahn-tah-OHR-ah): female flamenco singer

cantaores (kahn-tah-OHR-ehs): flamenco singers, all males or males and females

cante (KAHN-teh): flamenco song

castanets (kas-teh-NETS): musical instrument consisting of two small wood cups fastened to the thumb and clicked together with the other fingers

CE: abbreviation for *Common Era*; indicates a date from year 1 or later in the Western calendar

compás (kohm-PAHS): beat and rhythm of a song

duende (DOOWHEN-deh): strong feelings that inspire a flamenco singer

Egipto (eh-HEEP-toh): Spanish for *Egypt*

flamenco (flah-MEHN-koh): southern Spanish art form that incorporates song, dance, and music

flamencos (flah-MEHN-kohz): people who participate in flamenco

gracias (GRAH-see-ahs; *in Spain*: GRAH-thee-ahs): thank you

Granada (grah-NAH-dah): city in and capital of the province of Granada in Andalucía, Spain

Gustave Doré (goo-STAHV doh-RAY): French artist (1832–1883) who created images of life in southern Spain

Gypsy (JIP-see): member of the Roma

Janira Cordova (jan-EE-rah CORE-doh-vah): girl's full name

juerga flamenca (hoo-ER-gah flah-MEHN-kah): informal gathering where flamenco is performed; flamenco party

Moor (mor): Muslim Berber and Arab people of North Africa

Nicholas Cordova (NIK-oh-lahs CORE-doh-vah): boy's full name

¡olé! (oh-LAY): shout of approval and encouragement; bravo!

palmas (PAHL-mahs): rhythmic hand clapping

palmeros (pahl-MEHR-ohs): people who perform rhythmic hand clapping

patron saint (PAY-tren saynt): holy person regarded as a special guardian or protector

rasgueado (rahs-kay-AH-doh): rhythmic guitar-strumming technique in which the fingers are curled and then extended rapidly, one by one, across the strings

retablo (reh-TAH-bloh): religious painting on wood, stone, or metal

Roma (ROH-mah): group of people who originated in northern India; Gypsies

Sacromonte (sah-kroh-MOHN-teh): Sacred Mountain; neighborhood of hill caves in Granada, Spain

Sara-la-Kali (SAH-rah-luh-kah-LEE): Sara the Black; patron saint of the Roma

solo (SOH-loh): activity done alone, by one person

tocaor (toh-kah-OHR): male flamenco guitar player

tocaores (toh-kah-OHR-ehs): flamenco guitar players, all males or males and females

zapateado (sah-pah-teh-AH-doh; *in Spain*: thah-pah-teh-AH-doh): footwork that involves rapid stamping and tapping of the heels and soles of the shoes

Sources

Guardia, Maria (Maraquilla), and Carlos Arbejos. *Ardiendo y Echando Chispas.* Granada, Spain: Grupo Inmobiliario Romany, 2005.

Morca, Teodoro. *Becoming the Dance: Flamenco Spirit.* Dubuque, IA: Kendall Hunt Publishing, 1990.

Pohren, D. E. *The Art of Flamenco*. Sevilla, Spain: Society of Spanish Studies, 1972.

Schreiner, Claus, ed. *Flamenco: Gypsy Dance and Music from Andalusia.* Portland, OR: Amadeus Press, 1996.

Tomašević, Nebojša Bato, and Rajko Djurić. *Gypsies of the World.* New York: Henry Holt & Co., 1990.

Totton, Robin. *Song of the Outcasts: An Introduction to Flamenco*. Portland, OR: Amadeus Press, 2003.

Yoors, Jan. *The Gypsies of Spain.* New York: Macmillan, 1974.

¡Gracias!

My thanks go to all the wonderful people who made this magical journey into the world of flamenco possible. In Santa Fe, New Mexico: Maria Benitez, founder of the youth group of the Institute of Spanish Arts and teacher of the young artists at Flamenco's Next Generation; Janira and Nicholas Cordova; Danielle Cárdenas; Mikayla Garcia; Emily Grimm; Jaylena Luján; Alexandria and Isaiah Martínez; Caitlin Ortega; Miquela Sanchez-Wiegel; Simone Wimett; and all their faithful and gracious parents. In Albuquerque, New Mexico: Eva Encinias, founder of the National Institute of Flamenco. *Cantaores* Meagan Chandler, Francisco J. Orozco (Yiyi), and Alejandro País Iriart; *tocaores* Joaquín Gallegos and Chuscales, Mina, and their children; *bailaores* Domino Martinez, Julia Chacon, Keyana De Aguero, Carlos Menchaca, Illeana Gomez, and Jesús Muñoz; *flamencos* Karla Popolous, Keith Vizcarra, Gioia Tama, Carlos Lomas, Morgan Smith, Greg Gutin, Deborah Day, and Judy Chacon. In Spain: Paco Fernández and his family, Angel Galdo Fuentes, Pablo Guevara, Rocio Palacios Gonzalez and Christopher, Maite Olivares, Macarena Castilla Vargas, Jose Garrido Esteban, and Miriam Garrido Esteban. In Cuba: Eduardo Veitia of the Ballet Español de Habana. In New York: Patrick Lenaghan of The Hispanic Society of America and Louise May, who edited the book. And last but not least, my son Pablo Ancona, who worked with me on the book and accompanied me in Spain.

—*G.A.*